S.M.A.R.T Goals

Made Simple

10 Steps to Master Your Personal and Career Goals

By S.J. Scott

http://www.HabitBooks.com

2

January 2014
Copyright © 2014 S.J. Scott

Published by Archangel Ink

ISBN 1496154061
ISBN-13: 978-1496154064

Disclaimer

No part of this publication may be reproduced or transmitted in any form or by any means, mechanical or electronic, including photocopying or recording, or by any information storage and retrieval system, or transmitted by email without permission in writing from the publisher.

While all attempts have been made to verify the information provided in this publication, neither the author nor the publisher assumes any responsibility for errors, omissions, or contrary interpretations of the subject matter herein.

This book is for entertainment purposes only. The views expressed are those of the author alone, and should not be taken as expert instruction or commands. The reader is responsible for his or her own actions.

Adherence to all applicable laws and regulations, including international, federal, state, and local governing professional licensing, business practices, advertising, and all other aspects of doing business in the US, Canada, or any other jurisdiction is the sole responsibility of the purchaser or reader.

Neither the author nor the publisher assumes any responsibility or liability whatsoever on the behalf of the purchaser or reader of these materials.

Any perceived slight of any individual or organization is purely unintentional.

Table of Contents

How to Change Your Life with S.M.A.R.T. Goals

What do you *really* want from life?
We're all filled with dreams and aspirations.
Most long for fulfilling relationships. Some desire personal freedom. Others want fame and success. And some strive for profitable businesses.

Wherever your ambitions may lie, goal setting can get you there. On the other hand, the *wrong* goal can leave you feeling frustrated and unmotivated. When you set a goal that's *too lofty*, it's easy to give up when your dreams don't turn into reality.

We all have important milestones we'd like to reach. The trick is to create a plan and commit to it. Setting S.M.A.R.T. goals can help you do this.

It's easy to set S.M.A.R.T. goals. Simply write down a desired outcome on a piece of paper and create a deadline for achieving it. The *hard part* is taking action. As you know, the Internet is <u>full</u> of books that talk about setting goals. The problem? Most don't talk about the **daily actions** (or habits) required to achieve them.

In the following book, "**S.M.A.R.T. Goals Made Simple,**" you'll get a ten-step plan for setting and achieving your goals. Unlike other books, this book will teach you how to turn any idea into an *actionable* plan. Not only will you get an overview of S.M.A.R.T. goals, you'll also get a blueprint for turning them into daily routines.

Who Am I?

My name is S.J. Scott. I run the blog Develop Good Habits (http://www.developgoodhabits.com/).

The goal of my site is to show how *continuous* habit development can lead to a better life. Instead of lecturing you, I provide simple strategies that can be easily added to any busy life. It's been my experience that the best way to make a lasting change is to develop one quality habit at a time.

When I look back on my life, I'm able to trace every accomplishment back to one strategy—**goal setting**.

Whether it's running a marathon, backpacking through Europe, developing fulfilling relationships or building a successful online business, each of my major achievements started out as a simple goal.

As I've progressed in my personal development, I've come to realize that setting goals isn't about writing down an unreachable outcome on a piece of paper. Instead, it's about targeting a milestone that encourages daily action. My preferred method is to do it in the S.M.A.R.T. format *(Specific, Measurable, Attainable, Relevant and Time-bound).*

I set S.M.A.R.T. goals every three months (you'll learn why later on). Do I achieve all of them? Not at all. Instead, goals help me gain regular insight into what I *really* want from life and what actions can get me there. With this book, I hope to give you the same experience.

There's a lot we'll cover in *S.M.A.R.T. Goals Made Simple.* It's not hard to set a dynamic, inspiring goal. The trick is to follow it up with consistent action. In the following book, you'll learn how to set goals and then turn them into habits you'll follow every single day.

Sound interesting?

If so, keep reading to learn more.

What are S.M.A.R.T. Goals?

Before we get to the "meat" of this book, allow me to introduce a few concepts so we can all have the same frame of reference.

So what is a goal?

A goal is the desired outcome of an action or task.

People have different reasons for setting goals. Many want to improve their professional lives, challenge themselves or achieve specific dreams. The *value* of goal setting is that it helps you take an unclear idea and turn it into reality.

People who set goals are much more productive, according to numerous research studies. They also tend to be wealthier and more successful in their professional lives. Setting a goal and taking specific steps to achieve it will help you accomplish many things in your life.

So what are S.M.A.R.T. goals?

The key to effective goal-setting practice is to define your goals. It is not enough to say, *"I want to be rich."* This vague statement doesn't say anything about *how* and *when* the outcome will be achieved. In fact, it doesn't even clarify what you mean by the term "rich" and what, according to you, is "poor."

You can't create an action plan if you don't have a clear description of your desired outcome. The solution? Write down a goal with specific objectives. In keeping with the theme of this book, you need to create S.M.A.R.T. goals.

George Doran first used the S.M.A.R.T. acronym in the November 1981 issue of the *Management Review*. It stands for: **S**pecific, **M**easurable, **A**ttainable, **R**elevant and **T**ime-bound.
Here's how it works:

S: Specific

Specific goals answer your six "W" questions: *who, what, where, when, which and why.*

When you can identify each element, you'll know which tools (and actions) are required to reach a goal.

- Who: Who is involved?
- What: What do you want to accomplish?
- Where: Where will you complete the goal?
- When: When do you want to do it?
- Which: Which requirements and constraints might get in your way?
- Why: Why are you doing it?

Specificity is important because when you reach these milestones (date, location and objective), you'll know for certain you have achieved your goal.

M: Measurable

Measurable goals are defined with precise times, amounts, or other units—essentially anything that measures progress toward a goal.

Creating measurable goals makes it easy to determine if you have progressed from point A to point B. Measureable goals also help you figure out when you're headed in the right direction and when you're not. Generally, a measurable goal statement answers questions starting with "how," such as "how much," "how many" and "how fast."

A: Attainable

Attainable goals stretch the limits of what you think is possible. While they're not impossible to complete, they're often challenging and full of obstacles. The key to creating an attainable goal is to look at your current life and set an objective that seems *slightly* beyond your reach. That way, even if you fail, you still accomplish something of significance.

R: Relevant

Relevant goals focus on what you truly desire. They are the exact opposite of inconsistent or scattered goals. They are in harmony with everything that is important in your life, from success in your career to happiness with the people you love.

T: Time-bound

Time-bound goals have specific deadlines. You are expected to achieve your desired outcome before a target date. Time-bound goals are challenging and grounding. You can set your target date for today, or you can set it for a few months, few weeks or few years from now. The key to creating a time-bound goal is to set a deadline you'll meet by working backward and developing habits (more on this later).

S.M.A.R.T. goals are clear and well-defined. There is no doubt about the result you want to achieve. At its deadline, you'll know if you *have* or *haven't* achieved a particular goal.

Now, the *wording* of a goal is especially important. Focus on the right thing and you can do amazing things. When you focus on the wrong things, you may actually *lose* your motivation to achieve a goal. In the next section, we'll talk about two broad categories of goals. You'll find it's important to fully understand each before implementing the ten-step strategy we'll cover in the rest of the book.

Outcome Goals vs. Performance Goals

While a goal can be inspiring, it can also become detrimental if you fail to achieve it. I think this problem is caused by *how* a goal is written. In my opinion, most people focus too much on the outcome and too little on the process. Then when they fall short, they believe the whole thing was a waste of time.

To maximize your results, you need to understand the difference between "outcome goals" and "performance goals." Each has its own advantages and disadvantages, so let's talk about them both to see which one is right for you.

"Outcome Goals" are the goals people typically make. There is an intention to reach a specific milestone. Examples include making $___ per year, weighing ___ pounds or running a ___ time in your local 5K race.

The biggest advantage of an outcome goal is it makes you push yourself. There is no guarantee you'll reach a milestone, so you'll work extra hard and give maximum effort.

The disadvantage is an outcome goal often becomes an "all or nothing" proposition. Many people feel like failures when they don't reach their milestones—even if they've fully committed to the process. For many, outcome-based goals are de-motivating because it's easy to feel like a failure if you miss a milestone.

"Performance Goals" focus on tracking the *effort* and *actions* that go into a major accomplishment. For instance, let's say you're a sales professional who makes a six-figure yearly income. You know, on average, that you make 20 sales presentations per week to earn your current salary. Instead of 20, you set a goal of making 30 sales presentations per year. All things being equal, this will result in a 50 percent increase in your pay.

The advantage of performance-based goals is you focus on positive habit development instead of a number that's often arbitrary. Sometimes you have little control over a specific milestone. What you *can* control are the skills you develop and routines you follow on a daily basis.

The biggest disadvantage of a performance goal is it doesn't often work for someone who is getting started with goal setting. If you can't identify the actions required to reach a milestone, then you won't know whether a new habit is working or not. Another disadvantage is some people *need* that arbitrary number to get things done. They might not reach their milestones, but having a target number gives them enough motivation to stick to their goals.

EXAMPLE

The best way to illustrate the difference between these two types of goals is to provide examples from my own life. For many years, I've set outcome goals like these:

- "I will run under 3:00 at the Boston Marathon on April 15, 2013."
- "I will average 150 daily Kindle book sales from June 2013 to August 2013."
- "I will weigh 160 pounds by January 1, 2014."
- In 2014, I decided to switch things up and focus on setting performance goals like the following:
- "I will run a total of 510 miles from January 1 to March 31."
- "I will publish four Kindle books from January 1 to March 31."
- "I will write a total of 200,000 words from January 1 to March 31."
- "I will eat *no more* than 15 fast food/takeout meals from January 1 to March 31."
- "I will eat five daily servings of fruits and vegetables from January 1 to March 31."

Look closely at the difference between these two types of goals.

You'll see the performance goals are completely within my control, whereas you can fail with an outcome goal—even if you've worked hard. For instance, I ran a bad race at the Boston Marathon and came nowhere near my expected time of a sub three-hour race. [1]

The point here is that when you know specific actions can lead to a positive result, it's often better to focus on the routine instead of an arbitrary goal.

What Should You Pick?

I'll be the first to admit that performance goals aren't for everyone. I include them here more as an alternative to the standard way of doing things. There isn't a right answer—simply pick the category that provides the most motivation and inspiration.

My only piece of advice is to avoid the trap of tying your entire self-identity to an outcome you can't fully control. Not reaching a goal doesn't mean you're a bad person. It simply means you didn't reach an expected outcome.

Once you've decided to pick performance goals, outcome goals or a combination of both, take a look at your <u>entire</u> life and see what areas you'd like to improve. In the next section, we'll talk about how to do that.

---

[1] Of course my goal became extremely unimportant after the bombing. At the time, all I cared about was the safety of my friends and girlfriend.

Setting Goals for 7 Areas of Your Life

Goal setting isn't just about your job performance. You'll find that when you set goals for every area of your life, each goal supports the others and transforms you into a well-rounded person. It would be a mistake to focus on just one dimension (like finance or business) and neglect the other areas. Do this and you'll miss out on the major benefit of setting dynamic, long-term goals.

My advice is to set goals for all seven areas of your life:

- 1. Health
- 2. Relationships
- 3. Business
- 4. Finances
- 5. Leisure
- 6. Spirituality
- 7. Community

Take time to reflect on your life. Figure out what *truly* matters. Once you can identify what's important, you can create milestones that focus on leading a balanced life. For instance, here are a few examples of the seven areas written in S.M.A.R.T. goal format.

HEALTH

This area focuses on building a healthy lifestyle. Your goals might involve weight control, following a diet or becoming more physically active.

1.   Eat more vegetables and fruits: *"I will eat a minimum of five servings of fruits and vegetables daily by March 31 by mapping out my meals each week, going shopping twice a week and eating one to two servings per meal."*

2.   Cut down on processed food with high levels of sodium: *"Every time I purchase processed food, I will carefully read labels and buy only those foods with less than 200mg of sodium per serving."*

3.   3.Do regular workouts: *"I will work out a minimum of 30 minutes per day, three days per week by December 31."*

4.   4.Decrease the number of cigarettes you smoke: *"I will decrease the number of cigarettes I smoke to three per day by the end of this month. I will do this by carefully tracking each cigarette, understanding the triggers behind my urges and finding a way to replace this habit with a positive routine."*

5.   5. Healthy habit: *"By June 15, I will drink four large (16 ounces) glasses of water at work every day. I will do this by setting a reminder at night to fill up my bottles and take them with me when I leave for work in the morning."*

RELATIONSHIPS

You can set goals to improve relationships with your significant other, family members and friends. These goals might focus on your relationship with one person or your relationship with an entire group of people.

1. Improve communication with your spouse: *"I will identify three things I really love about my partner and tell her about them on Friday night. This will be done by scheduling a 30-minute block on Tuesday so I can reminisce about all the good times we've shared together."*

2. Spend quality time with your family: *"I will strengthen my bond with my family by taking them for a vacation at least once in six months. This will be accomplished by setting aside an hour each month during my review session and planning out future trip ideas."*

3. Improve communication with your spouse: *"By December 1, I will write down what I see my life being like with her ten years from now and ask her to do the same; then we'll compare our visions."*

4. Improving relationship with self: *"I will take one hour each week to do something I really enjoy. I will accomplish this by spending 30 minutes at the beginning of each month looking for things I want to do and finding out how much they cost. I will also set aside $20 from each paycheck so I can afford these fun activities."*

5. Strengthen family bonds: *"I will do five fun-filled weekend activities with my kids by June 1. I will do this by taking 30 minutes on Sunday (March 1) to research and schedule an activity that's both fun and educational."*

BUSINESS

Goals are an important part of building a business or a successful career. Whether it's improving a work-specific skill or focusing on outcomes that expand your business, you want to set challenging milestones that stretch the limit of what you think is possible.

1. Acquire new clients: *"I will acquire five new projects for my Web design consultancy through referrals, networking and social media marketing campaigns within two months."*

2. Increase productivity: *"I will limit my time on email correspondence to 30 minutes per day so I can work on the important projects delegated by my boss by December 31. I will do this by developing the 'inbox zero habit' and learning how to respond immediately to a message instead of procrastinating on it."*

3. Increase profits: *"I will increase profits by 20 percent this year by acquiring two new clients each week, finishing projects 10 percent faster and cutting $1,000 per month in expenditures."*

4. Expand your business: *"I will expand my business of e-learning digital classroom solutions by appointing two franchisees this year. I will do this by advertising my site on the International Franchising Association website and attending the national convention. "*

5. Improve job performance: *"I will redo my company's website design by May 1. This will be done by finding the right graphic designer and Web programmer, then using their skills to create a dynamic visual presentation."*

FINANCES

The finance category includes a number of important areas of your life: saving for retirement or a down payment on a home, planning a vacation and becoming debt-free.

1. Regular savings: *"I will save 10 percent of every paycheck and invest it in index funds through my 401k."*
2. Living within a budget: *"I will set a spending limit of $4,000 every month. Then I'll track every expense and make sure I'm spending less than this amount."*
3. Spend wisely: *"I will make a list of essentials to buy every month. Then I'll look for bargains online (for at least one hour) before I go shopping at the mall."*
4. Eliminate debt on credit cards: *"I will pay the outstanding balance of $5,000 on my credit cards in installments and become totally debt-free in three years. This will be done by asking each credit card company to reduce my APR. Then I'll systematically pay off the cards with the highest interest rates down to the lowest interest rates."*
5. Plan for retirement: *"I will save $20,000 every year for my retirement fund of $500,000 at the end of 25 years. This will be done by having $769 automatically withdrawn from each paycheck."*

LEISURE

Leisure activities are as significant as business or family goals. You might choose to reserve moments for exclusive "me time." Or, you can spend some time with your family/friends for relaxation. Some potential leisure activities include travel, adventure and learning new hobbies such as dance, music, cooking or painting.

1. Family fun: *"I will enjoy the Maid of the Mist boat ride in Niagara Falls with my family by August 31. On Saturday (March 1), I will spend two hours planning this trip and making all the necessary reservations."*

2. Travel: *"I will take a cruise to Alaska with my friends by August 1, 2014. On Saturday (March 1), I will spend the entire day discussing the cruise with my friends and then book the trip with my travel agent."*

3. 3.Learn new skills: *"I will learn rock climbing this summer and climb a simple Class 4 at Yosemite. This will be accomplished by joining the local climbing class that meets on Saturdays during the wintertime. Then I'll join a week-long course in the summer to exponentially develop my climbing skills."*

4. Cultivate hobbies: *"I will spare three hours every week to learn and practice watercolor painting. This will be done by eliminating unimportant habits—like watching T.V."*

5. Outdoor activities: *"I will spend at least one hour outdoors every day tending my garden, jogging or power walking. This will be done by blocking out an hour for each day during my weekly review and setting a daily reminder to get outdoors."*

SPIRITUALITY

For many people, spiritual well-being is as important as their physical or mental health. The word "spirituality" takes on a different meaning to each of us. It could include activities like meditation, prayer, yoga or anything else that helps you experience peace of mind.

1. Meditate regularly: *"I will meditate for 20 minutes each morning. This habit will be developed by setting an alert 7:20 a.m. using the Mind Jogger app."*

2. Being thankful: *"I will take five minutes each day to give thanks for everything that's good in my life. I will develop this habit by setting aside time right before my lunch to remember what's important."*

3. Feel compassion: *"I will develop forgiveness and feel compassion every day toward all people. While I might not do this all the time, I will set a reminder each day to think of one person I should forgive for hurting me."*

4. Prayer: *"I will set aside 10 minutes each day and pray to God. This habit will be added to my nighttime routine—before I go to sleep."*

5. Spiritual journey: *"I will go to Mecca this year during Ramadan. Starting this Saturday (March 1), I will spend 30 minutes with my family planning the trip. I will continue doing this activity for the next three months."*

COMMUNITY

Harmonious relations within your community are as important as physical health, mental and emotional well-being, and financial security. Deciding to volunteer for community services can also promote personal growth and self-esteem. Not only does it reduce stress, it also forces you to think of others instead of yourself.

1. Volunteer at a hospital: *"I will volunteer at a local hospital for three hours every week. This will be done by*

registering with the volunteer organization, scheduling the three hours and blocking out this time in my schedule."

2. Pro bono coaching: *"I will offer pro bono coaching to one disadvantaged student in every quarter. The student will be found during my weekly volunteer work on Saturdays. I will get to know the students and identify the one who has the most potential."*

3. Monthly donations: *"I will donate $100 every month to the 'Help a Child' project in India. This will be done by setting up an automatic withdrawal from my bank account."*

4. Help kids in need: *"This summer, I will spend ten hours (each week) with kids in need by reading books to them, providing healthy and fresh food to them, and building a playground or creating a community garden for them."*

Hopefully looking at these seven examples gave you an idea of how to set S.M.A.R.T. goals for a balanced life. You don't *always* need to focus on all of them at once, but it *is* important to do something every year to grow as a person. You'll find that when you focus on different things, they'll often feed off one another and help you think of additional strategies you can implement.

As an example, I do my best "business thinking" during my runs and walks. Sure, these activities are about improving my health, but they're also great for clearing my mind and figuring out solutions to specific obstacles.

How many goals should you have at once?

My advice is to **focus on five areas of your life** at any given point. Look at the seven areas we've discussed and identify what's most important to you right now. Then create goals that tap into an outcome you find both challenging and exciting.

Now, I'll be the first to admit that writing down a goal isn't the same as achieving it. The only way you'll get results is to take action. The funny thing? The "action" doesn't need to be a monumental thing. Instead, it's better to take baby steps on a daily basis. In other words, you can achieve any goal by focusing on your habits. And that's what we'll talk about in the next section.

5 Steps for Turning S.M.A.R.T. Goals into Habits

I have a major bone to pick with most goal-setting books. They do a good job of covering topics like writing down goals, putting them into the future tense and visualizing them. Yet they rarely talk about the **daily process** of *actually* achieving them. The unpleasant truth is that while setting goals can be fun, the achievement part often requires a daily slog of repeating the same action over and over.

Ultimately, it's your **habits** that will make or break your goal achievement efforts.

Really, success comes down to the choices you make every day. Will you structure time around goals? Or will you let distractions prevent you from taking consistent action? The choice you make here will ultimately determine your level of success.

There are no secrets to completing a goal.

In fact, it's a straightforward, five-step process:

Step #1: Turn Your Goal into a Project

Odds are your goal requires multiple actions, so you need to turn it into a step-by-step project. The easiest way to do this is to look at the target date and work your way backward. Visualize reaching this milestone. What did you do to get to this point? Once you identify the actions, you simply put them down into a simple, step-by-step list.

For instance, let's say you create this goal: *"I will complete the Chicago Marathon as my first marathon on October 12th, 2014."*

To make this happen, you'd need to break down this fitness goal into the following plan:

1. Find out the date when the registration starts for the marathon.
2. Schedule a reminder to sign up on that day.
3. Sign up for the Chicago Marathon.
4. Read books/articles on how to create a marathon training plan.
5. Create a week-by-week plan with an emphasis on increasing your long run.
6. Start tracking your daily running to stay accountable to this goal.
7. Run one or two half-marathons to gauge your overall level of fitness.
8. Decide if you're ready to tackle the full marathon distance with two months to go. (August 12th.)
9. Book a round-trip ticket to Chicago.
10. Book a hotel room for the weekend of October 12.
11. Write down a packing list for what you'll need.

12. Pack for the marathon and hop on the plane.
13. Go to the marathon expo, pick up race instructions and figure out the best time in the morning to leave for the race.
14. Wake up on October 12 and make your way to the starting line.
15. Run the Chicago Marathon.
16. Drink a tall glass of beer while wearing your finisher's medal.

Sure you could make the argument that the only "action" required to reach this goal is to run four to five times perweek. The important lesson here is everything can (and should) be turned into a step-by-step project. You'll find that chunking a goal into small steps makes it an achievable process.

Step #2: Schedule Time Every Day to Work on Goals

Notice how I said "schedule time," not "find time." Many people make the mistake of trying to squeeze goals into their busy days. Often this leads to failure because the urgent (but not important) activities have a way of taking up most of your day.

How long you spend on a goal depends on the time that's required. Some only require a few minutes each week, while others require hours of your day (that's why it's important to understand the time commitment of each goal.) Figure out how much time you'll need for each task and schedule them into your week.

For instance, let's continue with our Chicago Marathon example. An important part of any marathon program is completing a long run every two weeks, which builds up to a distance of 20 to 22 miles. This is a major time commitment for many people. To achieve this goal, you'll need to block out large parts of your day for running.

Regardless of *when* you work on a goal, a helpful trick is to create a schedule where you do the same activity at the same time every day. That way when you reach that hour, you'll get used to following this habit without experiencing a lot of internal resistance. In fact, the more routine a goal becomes, the more you'll do it on a consistent basis.

Step #3: Turn Goals into Important Tasks

We've already talked about why it's important to make time instead of finding time. Unfortunately, that's easier said than done. We all have those busy schedules full of activities that conflict with one another. The solution? Start your day by working on goals first thing in the morning.

A few years back, Leo Babauta talked about a concept called Most Important Tasks (MITs) (http://zenhabits.net/purpose-your-day-most-important-task/). The idea here is to identify the tasks that have the biggest impact on your life or business and do them the moment you wake up.

Start each morning by identifying the three tasks that need to be completed by the end of the day. Two should relate to a current project and one should be part of a long-term goal. Moreover, one of the three MITs should be a habit that you perform on a daily basis.

Using the marathon example, you could start each day with a run. Then after showering, eating a quick breakfast and driving to work, you'd spend the rest of the morning working on the projects that have the biggest impact on your career. And then you would end the day by focusing on the activities that are important, but aren't directly tied to long-term goals (like answering email).

Step #4: Schedule Time for Single Actions

Oddly enough, many people don't have a problem with completing the daily activities. Instead, they're often bogged down by the single actions that are important, but not immediately urgent. A quick fix for this is to schedule time each week to complete a number of single actions.

When you schedule time for this depends on you. Some people like to set aside a single multi-hour block each week to tackle their personal projects. Others prefer the *Getting Things Done* approach where they batch tasks according to the action that needs to be completed, such as making phone calls, running errands and doing tasks at work. Simply find what works best for you and schedule time to complete these actions.

Step #5: Track Your Goals

The key to achieving a goal is consistency. You have to follow through on a daily basis and also complete those single-action items. Focusing on MITs can help you tackle the most important parts of your goal, but <u>tracking</u> your goals on a daily basis makes a big difference.

What you track depends on the nature of each goal. This goes back to the "M" part of your S.M.A.R.T. goals—create measurements for every outcome you'd like to achieve. That means you should identify precise time frames, amounts or units that *quantify* your progression toward a goal.

To illustrate this point, let's go back to the marathon example. Depending on your fitness level, most runners average 35 to 50 weekly miles when they're training for a marathon. That means you'd need a tool that measures your weekly mileage. Some people do this with a training log, while others prefer mobile phone apps like Runner's Log (http://bit.ly/1cHzi6z).

The type of goal really doesn't matter. Nowadays almost anything can be quantified, measured and tracked with simple-to-use software (we'll talk about my favorites in a later section). What's important is to measure your progress on a daily basis.

Successful Goals = Successful Habits

I'll admit it's not glamorous to repeat the same action day in and day out, but that's the *real* secret to achieving a long-term goal. Think of yourself like The

Tortoise in the classic fable: "Slow and steady wins the race." If you commit to practicing positive habits every day, you <u>will</u> successfully complete your goals.

When a goal turns into a habit, you don't have to "force" yourself to do it every day. Instead it'll become a natural part of your day like eating, brushing your teeth or driving a car.

Okay, we've come to the end of the S.M.A.R.T. goal overview.

Now it's time to jump into the strategy portion of this book. In the next section, we'll kick things off with the first step of our ten-step plan for achieving any goal.

Step 1: Buy a Goal Book

Dr. Gail Matthews, a psychology professor at Dominican University of California, has done a lot of interesting research on setting goals. She found that people who do three core activities are 33 percent *more* successful than people who keep goals in their heads:

1. Write down their goals.
2. Share them with friends.
3. Send weekly updates about their goals.

According to Dr. Matthews, accountability, commitment and writing down one's goals are the three best strategies for successfully achieving a goal. Her findings back up many other cases where the people who write down a desired outcome are more likely to do it.

There are two methods for recording goals.

The first is the pen-and-paper approach. In my opinion, this is a better method than relying on technology because writing down a goal embeds it into your subconscious mind and stores it in your long-term memory. If you write (and review) your goals every day, you'll get a constant reminder on the importance of taking action.

Typing up your goals is an extension of this first method. Some people (like me) have horrible chicken-scratch handwriting. If you think better with a computer, then this method can be a substitute for the pen-and-paper approach.

The next option is to use software or a mobile app. This works similarly to the pen-and-paper approach. The difference is you can store this information digitally and have it accessible on a tablet, mobile phone or desktop computer.

Again I recommend going with the written goal option. This approach is similar to *journaling.* There are a lot of benefits to writing down a goal. Do it this way and you:

- Gain clarity about what you really want.
- Can elaborate on the actions that are required.
- Make a plan of how you'll achieve them.
- Understand the obstacles and challenges that need to be overcome.
- Identify the resources you currently possess.

One of the reasons I like written goals is you can pin them on your wall and carry them wherever you go. You can also put them in a notebook and keep track of the individual parts of each project.

How to Create Your Goals Book

I know many people use Moleskine notebooks for goals, but I prefer the Avery Flexi-View One-Inch Binder (http://www.developgoodhabits.com/avery) because it's lightweight, easy to carry around and can be customized according to your goals and projects.

You can do a number of things with a binder like this:

- Store up to 175 sheets.
- Keep track of your goals with specific action items and deadlines.
- Find specific goals quickly without needing to boot up a computer.
- Create different sections in your binder to organize and monitor your goals.
- Schedule important tasks, meetings and follow-ups that need to completed for each goal. These can then be added to a daily/weekly to-do list for immediate follow-up.
- Add a separate section for life lists and long-term goals (more on these later).

Maintaining a dedicated goal book is a powerful habit. Not only is it useful for daily review, it's also a great motivator for those times when nothing seems to go right. Finally, it can act as a filter when a new opportunity pops up. Simply compare it to your existing goals to see if it's worth pursuing or not.

After purchasing a goal book, you'll want to add items to it. In the next section, we'll talk about the first item to include—your life list.

Step 2: Create a Life List

It's a commonplace experience to set a goal and fail to follow through on it. Sometimes this happens because a person's long-term plans have changed. Other times it's because the person doesn't know what they *truly* want from life.

The people who consistently achieve their goals understand the relationship between motivation and accomplishment. Instead of setting arbitrary outcomes, they can clearly describe what they desire and then use this information to spur themselves into action.

It might sound trite, but the simplest way to identify what you want is to imagine your future self lying on your deathbed. *What are the things you'd regret not being able to do? What are the things you'd be most proud to have achieved? What relationships did you most enjoy? What experiences gave meaning to your daily existence? What lives did you improve through your actions and efforts?*

The point behind this exercise?

When you start at the end, you can reverse-engineer the rest of your life. The "death bed analogy" is the simplest way to know what's really important and what will ultimately be a waste of your time. The items you write down from this experience will become your "life list" (or bucket list).

There's a lot that can go into a life list. Everything comes down to your perspective and experiences. So it makes sense to only include the items that are personally significant.

Get started by answering these questions:

- What are your heartfelt desires for you and your family?
- What have you always dreamed of doing?
- What activities make you feel inspired and driven?
- What thoughts give you goose bumps while imagining them?
- What things have you always wanted to own?
- What uplifts you spiritually?

Use these questions to generate a number of potential goals. The key here is to not *censure* yourself. Allow your subconscious mind to identify the important things in your life. Keep adding to this list by identifying what you've always dreamed of achieving. Like goals, a life list shouldn't focus on one part of your life (like your career). Instead, it should help you become a balanced person. That means it's important to include all seven areas of goal setting. Here are a few examples for each area:

HEALTH

1. Become a Zumba fitness instructor.
2. Master ten yoga poses.
3. Maintain a bikini body all year long by working out regularly.
4. Become a complete vegan.
5. Run a marathon in all 50 states.

RELATIONSHIPS

1. Become a good role model for your children.
2. Master 20 recipes so you and your spouse can cook together.
3. Make a scrapbook of your memorable moments with friends and family.
4. Go on a whitewater rafting trip with your family.
5. Take a weeklong cruise with your parents on the Danube River.

BUSINESS

1. Build a successful franchise business.
2. Increase yearly inventory turnover ten times.
3. Become the chief financial officer (CFO) of your company.
4. Start an online coaching program as a life coach.
5. Receive an award for outstanding business accomplishments.

FINANCES

1. Build a 401K that has more than $500,000 in funds.

2. Pay for all of your children to attend college.
3. Master the fundamentals of stock market trading.
4. Buy a vacation home on an island.
5. Become financially literate and fully understand all investment strategies.

LEISURE

1. Take a trip in a hot-air balloon.
2. Go on a SCUBA diving trip with your friends.
3. Ride the world's largest Ferris wheel.
4. Travel to five other continents.
5. Become fluent in the French language.

SPIRITUALITY

1. Meet the Dalai Lama or the Pope.
2. Do missionary work in Africa for one year.
3. Truly forgive anyone who has angered you in the past.
4. Visit Mecca.
5. Master the ideal of living in the present moment.

COMMUNITY

1. Donate blood every three months.
2. Tithe 10 percent of your income to a good cause.
3. Become a "Big Brother" or "Big Sister."
4. Get your family member to volunteer *at least* once per month.
5. Sponsor a scholarship.

There's a lot you can do with a life list. This is one of those rare opportunities where you can dream big and not run the risk of public embarrassment. If you secretly imagine winning *American Idol,* then write it down! You're the only one who will see this list, so let your imagination run wild.

Creating a life list can be a very positive experience. The responses you give here will help define your inner values and the specific goals you'd like to achieve in the immediate future. So let's talk about how to do that.

Step 3: Write Down Yearly Goals

Everyone has their personal preference when it comes to long-term goals. Some think big by focusing on a five-year plan; others like to take them one year at a time, and a few prefer the immediacy of focusing on the next three months. I think it's best to focus on a set of major goals broken down into years and quarters.

I often compare goals to a business plan. They're a projection of what you'd like to achieve in the next 12 months. You have a general "idea" of what you want to do, but you're also flexible enough to change plans along the way.

Creating a S.M.A.R.T. yearly goal is simple enough. Starting now, look at the end of the calendar for this year and think about what you'd like to achieve. This could include things like:

- The exact salary you'd like to make.
- The revenue your business should generate.

- The major athletic accomplishments you'd like to make.
- The trips and vacations you'd like to do with your family.
- The volunteering events you'd like to do.
- The ways you'd like to grow spiritually.
- The relationships you'd like to develop or deepen.

Write these down in S.M.A.R.T. format, but don't worry too much about their specific outcome. Remember to treat each goal like a business plan instead of a mandatory milestone you need to reach. In a way, these goals act like a bridge between a life list and the short-term goals you should be working on daily. Then you'll take this list and break it down further into three-month goals, so let's talk about how to do that.

Step 4a: Focus on Setting Three-Month Goals

L ife lists and yearly goals are often nebulous, "someday" items. The main reason I didn't spend much time on that previous section is because long-term goals are constantly shifting. What seems urgent today often isn't important next month. The strategy that works *for me* is to take a yearly goal and to break it down into three month (or quarterly) goals.

Why Three-Month Goals?

Let's face it. Our world is fast-paced and constantly shifting. In order to capitalize on all these changes, it's often better to create goals for the short-term. While it's important to set those yearlong milestones, you'll find that immediate goals usually lead to consistent action and a high level of motivation.

It's also been my experience that lengthy goals (i.e.; anything over six months) are often de-motivational. When you know an outcome is months away, it's easy to procrastinate on taking consistent action. You keep putting off your goals, promising you'll work on them *next week*. Next thing you know—it's a year later and nothing has been accomplished.

How to Create a Three-Month Goal

The best way to get started with a yearly goal is to work backwards. Think about 12 months from now. What's the specific milestone you'd like to reach? Once you've identified this outcome, break down the process into four parts—each will be worked on during a separate quarter.

A great example of this is how I go about setting goals for publishing Kindle books. For 2014, I've set a yearlong goal of publishing 10 to 12 books. (My primary goal is 12, but I'd still be happy with 10.) That's a maximum of three books per quarter or one per month. When I apply this strategy to a three month increments, it would look like this:

- Quarter 1: Publish books #1 to #3
- Quarter 2: Publish books #4 to #6
- Quarter 3: Publish books #7 to #9
- Quarter 4: Publish books #10 to #12

Perhaps an even better example would be losing weight. Think of those T.V. shows where a person needs to lose *hundreds* of pounds. I'd think this would be hard to do if they were forced to think about a year's worth of effort. However if you broke down the challenge into four quarters, the goal would become more manageable:

- Quarter 1: Lose 25 pounds (total loss of 25 pounds).
- Quarter 2: Lose 25 pounds (total loss of 50 pounds).
- Quarter 3: Lose 25 pounds (total loss of 75 pounds).
- Quarter 4: Lose 25 pounds (total loss of 100 pounds).

As you can see, the main benefit of this strategy is you're not overwhelmed by the uphill battle that reaching this goal requires. Instead you break it down into doable chunks, which are then further broken down into monthly, weekly, daily and hourly activities (more on this later).

Since this book emphasizes S.M.A.R.T. goal setting, let's show how the above would be written in that format:

- On March 31, I will be at 225 pounds, having lost 25 pounds in the last three months by tracking each of my meals, eating five to seven servings of fruits/vegetables each day and exercising a minimum of 40 minutes per day, five days per week.
- On June 30, I will be at 200 pounds, having lost 25 pounds in the last three months by tracking each of my meals, eating five to seven servings of fruits/vegetables each day and exercising a minimum of 40 minutes per day, five days per week.
- On September 30, I will be at 175 pounds, having lost 25 pounds in the last three months by tracking each of my meals, eating five to seven

servings of fruits/vegetables each day and exercising a minimum of 40 minutes per day, five days per week.

• On December 31, I will be at 150 pounds, having lost 25 pounds in the last three months by tracking each of my meals, eating five to seven servings of fruits/vegetables each day and exercising a minimum of 40 minutes per day, five days per week.

As you can see, this is how you take a long-term goal and turn it into an actionable plan. The one thing you probably noticed is I repeated the "action plan" in each goal. If this was a true three-month S.M.A.R.T. goal, you'd begin each quarter by seeing what strategies have worked and then using them to create a new set of goals.

The question:

How do you create an actionable three-month plan?

That's what we'll cover in the next section.

Step 4b: Create Quarterly Goals by Implementing Five Actions

There's a simple process for turning a yearly goal into an actionable plan. Here is a simple five-part action plan for getting started.

Action 1: Review Each Yearly Goal

Your life is constantly changing. What was important a few months ago might not seem all that interesting right now. That's why it's important to start each quarter by going through your yearly goals to see if they're still relevant.

Get started by thinking of what you've done in the past quarter. Ask yourself the following questions for each goal:

- What have I achieved so far?
- Is there a way to build on my success?
- What specific strategies got me to this point?
- What obstacles did I overcome?
- Is it still motivating and exciting?

- Should I eliminate this goal?
- Is there a related (or even different) goal I should add?

This exercise is important because many people often don't take the time to examine their goals. Instead, they continue to plod on because they made the commitment to follow through. By examining each goal, you can take the lessons from the last three months and apply them to the goals you'll set for the next quarter.

Action 2: Prioritize Your Life

Even if you have multiple goals, there will be times when it's important to focus on one or two key areas. This is especially true if you have a looming deadline in the next three months.

After examining each goal, prioritize them in order of urgency. That way you'll know where to focus your efforts when pressed for time.

For instance, let's say in the previous quarter you focused on achieving a major athletic accomplishment—like running a marathon. During a second-quarter evaluation, you realized that your body needs rest and recovery, so you decide to put "health/fitness" goals on the back burner and focus on spending time with family. Sure, you'll still exercise, but it won't be as critical as achieving your family goals.

Action 3: Focus on Five (or Fewer) Goals

Not only is it important to focus on a few key areas every quarter, it's equally important to limit the total number of goals you have. My advice is to stick to a maximum of five at a time. Again, this is all about sticking to what's important. If you try to do too much, your focus will be divided as you struggle to do too many things.

Action 4: Set Deadlines and Time Frames

We've already discussed the effectiveness of setting time frames in the process of S.M.A.R.T. goal setting, but when it comes to quarterly goals, it's best to create artificial deadlines that come within the next three months. There are two ways to do this.

In some cases, you are not the one setting your deadline. You might have to attend an already-scheduled event or complete a project with a deadline assigned by your boss. When there's a specific deadline, you'll need to account for this in your quarterly goal and make sure you're leaving enough time to get it successfully completed.

For some goals, the only deadline is the end of the quarterly period. What you do then is create a metric that's challenging, but doable. Simply think of the yearly goal, decide what makes a good milestone and then pick a target metric for the next three months.

Action 5: Create Action-Oriented S.M.A.R.T. Goals

We've already covered S.M.A.R.T. goal setting, so I won't rehash its principles. Instead, I recommend you take each of the five quarterly goals and break them down into short-term outcomes.

As an example, here's what an actionable goal would look like for each of the seven areas of life:

HEALTH

1. "I will not eat any fast food through July 1."
2. "I will eat three or more home-cooked dinners each week through August 1 instead of eating takeout."
3. "I will fit into my favorite black dress again by February 1."

RELATIONSHIPS

1. "We will celebrate our fifth wedding anniversary in Paris from October 1 through October 10."
2. "We will schedule one date night every other weekend."
3. "I will hug my girlfriend (or wife) each morning and say that I love her."

BUSINESS

1. "I will complete a book proposal and submit it to 25 publishers by February 1."
2. "I will hire a virtual personal assistant by July 31."

3. "I will read two career-oriented books by December 31."

FINANCES

1. "I will increase my income 10 percent by doing part-time consulting work in the evenings by May 1."
2. "I will add $5,000 to my house down payment savings by December 31."
3. "I will research stocks and invest $2,500 in the market by May 31."

SPIRITUALITY

1. "I will pray for 10 minutes every day until March 1st."
2. "I will go to an inner awakening retreat in India in December this year."
3. "I will go on a weeklong retreat to Sedona, AZ from October 4 to October 10."

LEISURE

1. "We will visit Disney World for our youngest son's sixth birthday."
2. "My spouse and I will enjoy a weekend getaway the third weekend of every month."
3. "I will go on a bike ride with my family every Saturday morning for the entire summer."

COMMUNITY/SOCIAL

1. "I will volunteer at a homeless shelter every weekend."

2. "I will donate old clothes to a battered women's shelter by the end of this month."
3. "I will mentor one person at work every three months."

It's really not that hard to turn a yearly goal into a quarterly process. Start by taking time to analyze what you've successfully done in the past; then use this information to set specific milestones for the next three months. Rinse and repeat for each of the five goals to get a blueprint for taking action on a daily basis.

So, how do you turn a quarterly goal into a day-to-day process?

In the next section, we'll talk about how to do this.

Step 5a: Turn Quarterly Goals into Action Plans

The easiest part of goal setting is writing everything down. What's difficult is *taking action*. Once you've created a goal, you need to work backward and figure out how you'll get to your desired outcome.

The key to successful goal achievement is turning your goals into projects.

You start by creating a goal like this: *"I will give a dynamic 30-minute keynote presentation at the national conference on July 1, 2014."* Then you work your way backward from this date and map out the steps needed to get to this point. Usually this means creating an action plan with a deadline for each component.

Get started by chunking down each of your quarterly goals into monthly, weekly, daily and hourly blocks of time. One of the easiest ways to do this is to create a project list and turn it into a series of mini-milestones that you accomplish over the next three months.

EXAMPLE:

Using the above example ("giving a keynote presentation"), let's break it down into a simple process.

1. Pick a dynamic topic to present at the conference.
2. Pitch it to the event organizers and make sure they're happy with the topic.
3. Mind map an overview of what the presentation will cover.
4. Talk to the "target audience" and find out their current challenges/obstacles.
5. Collect related data, metrics and statistics.
6. Organize the information into a logical order.
7. Create a rough draft of the presentation.
8. Get feedback from colleagues, mastermind group members and friends, ask for their input.
9. Write the second, third and final versions of the presentation.
10. Practice it until you're comfortable with the material.
11. Give the presentation.

Notice how this list contains a blend of single actions and habits? That means not only do you need to complete each item, you'll also need to set aside blocks of time each day to practice your presentation. Obviously, your goals will be different. The key point here is to start with the end goal in mind and then work your way backward until you identify all of the actions that need to be completed.

Now, one of the major problems people have with creating project lists is they can't think of every component that's required. While some people like creating linear lists (like a project list), others prefer the process of mind mapping. In the next section, we'll go over this concept.

Step 5b: Brainstorm Project Ideas Using Mind Mapping

Mind mapping is an alternative (or additional) way to create a project list. Instead of writing everything down in a step-by-step format, you use a two-dimensional (often colorful) diagram that presents thoughts, ideas and plans in non-linear fashion. This is called a **mind map**.

Mind maps engage both hemispheres of the brain. As a result, they are a powerful tool for planning, organizing and communicating a long-term goal.

With a mind map, you can also make an honest assessment of your skills, abilities and available resources. Anything you can do to come up with a working strategy can put you on the road to completing a goal in a timely fashion.

It's not hard to create a mind map.

Here is a simple seven-step process:

I: Schedule Mind-Mapping Time

Set aside 30 to 45 minutes for each major goal. This time isn't set in stone because some goals require a minimal amount of planning, while others force you to think of many different variables. My rule of thumb is to dedicate at least half an hour for each of your goals.

II: Ask Four Key Questions

Mind maps start with a deep understanding of each of your three-month goals. Get started by asking these four questions.

- "What actions are required to reach these three-month goals?"
- "What are my current strengths and resources?"
- "What obstacles will get in the way of my success?"
- "What additional skills do I need to develop to accomplish these goals?"

Take a look at your past experiences with each yearly goal. Think of what you've learned from both your successes *and* failures. Then use this information as you create a mind map for each goal.

III: Start Mind Mapping

Go to your local office supply store and purchase a pad of drawing paper (or use the software that's recommended below). I prefer this option over normal paper because you'll have more room to write down everything you'll need to achieve a goal.

To get an idea of how a mind map looks, take a look at a few different examples courtesy of Google. (http://bit.ly/1fNtjKP)

Once you have the right tool(s), you'll start mind mapping. Here are a few ways to map out your ideas:

- **Use keywords, lines, colors and images to express ideas**. A mind map is a visual expression of interconnected information that is easy to review and recall. Your brain processes information associatively, so connecting ideas in a non-linear fashion will help you determine what needs to be done to successfully complete a goal.

- **Evolve your ideas naturally.** Start with a simple one-sentence goal or thought. For a three-month goal, it helps to put the goal in the center of the diagram and then surround the center with sub-centers that explain various mini-projects/ideas that need to be accomplished.

- **Use a relevant keyword/image for each sub-center**. When using keywords, use lowercase letters as they are easier to remember. The center is connected to the sub-centers by spokes. You can use different colors to highlight different themes and associations.

- **Draw arrows to elaborate on each idea.** From each sub-center, create an arrow that branches out. Use the arrow to explain what needs to be accomplished. You can add new ideas and actions as the project evolves. This diagram is free flowing, so you can delete/add items as you work toward completing these three-month goals.

IV: Identify Challenges

An important part of mind mapping is identifying the challenges that might hinder your completion of a goal. Specifically there are three primary types of challenges:

1. **Outcome Obstacles:** Goals must be consistent with your long-term plans and what's *really* important. If they're in conflict, then you probably won't succeed.

2. For instance, if you're pursuing goals simply to please someone else, then you won't have the internal motivation needed to take action on a daily basis. My advice is to avoid creating goals simply because they sound good on paper.

3. **Fears:** Fear of failure or some other internal feelings such as self-doubt, lack of confidence or procrastination can pull you back from wholeheartedly going after a goal.

Dedicate an area for your fears during the mind-mapping process. Take time to think about what the "limiting beliefs" are that hold you back from going after a goal. Then come up with a few possible solutions. Odds are you'll discover that it's not hard to overcome a fear once you've clearly identified why you feel a certain way.

4. **Roadblocks:** Sometimes external factors get in the way of achieving your goals. When facing external roadblocks, it's important to identify the actual problem. Simply review each potential roadblock and think of how you'll respond if it comes up.

V: Avoid Censuring Yourself

Write down ideas as soon as they emerge without being judgmental or analytical. Sure, some might not seem that important, but they might lead to a secondary thought that has an amazing impact on your ability to complete a goal. Allow yourself to follow through on every idea. Expand each one into branches and sub-branches and then go from there.

VI: Segment the Mind-Mapping Process

Our brain works best in five- to seven-minute bursts. During these bursts, capture as many ideas as you can and record those ideas rapidly using keywords, symbols, images and colors. Take a break for a few minutes and then go back to the diagram. Do this enough times to make sure you're fully elaborating on every possible idea.

VII: Turn Mind Maps into Action Plans

After brainstorming ideas, turn them into specific action lists. This goes back to the previous section. Simply think of what tasks need to be completed in chronological order and then schedule them in your calendar for follow-up.

That's really all you need to do to create a mind map. It's a simple exercise that only takes 30 minutes to complete. Do it for all five goals and you'll generate an avalanche of ideas with this multi-dimensional process.

Mind-Mapping Resources

While I prefer the old pen-and-paper approach to mind mapping, many people like the technology approach to expanding on their ideas. Here are a few tools you can use for this process:

1. iMindMap (http://thinkbuzan.com/)is software developed by Tony Buzan, who many consider the inventor of mind mapping. It takes a slightly different approach to mind mapping than other software. While iMindMap is a premium product, you can try it free with a seven-day trial.

2. FreeMind (http://cnet.co/1fi0hlH)is a Java-based program with an extensive support wiki (http://bit.ly/1d4SNDR) that explains how to operate the application, create your own keyboard shortcuts and maximize your mind-mapping experience.

3. MindMeister (http://www.mindmeister.com/) is the most simplistic online mind-mapping application. You can instantly create a basic mind map by using nodes, arrows and insert keys. It's fully customizable with node colors and font sizes, and you can share your mind maps with other collaborators.

Mind-mapping apps are available for iPad, iPhone and Android-based tablets. The most popular apps are the mobile versions of MindMeister or iMindMap. Plus, you can also look for these competing apps which offer a similar mind mapping experience: MindJet, MindMaps Lite, SimpleMind, Mind Mapping Free, MindMemo, MindGenius and MindMapper.

Simply do a search in the app store to find one that works for you.

It doesn't matter what device you use to create a mind map, there are plenty of tools that can be used to expand on your ideas and map out the steps you'll need to take to reach a specific goal.

Now, one of the limitations of project lists and mind maps is you often don't know *what* needs to be done. This is true if you've set a goal that requires you to learn a new skill. In the next section, we'll talk about a simple strategy to pick up the knowledge and skills for a brand new goal.

Step 5c: Learn New Skills for a Specific Goal

Sometimes it's not enough to plan out a project because you don't know how to do something. The solution is simple—you must take the time to learn the required skill.

Refer back to the list of steps for a project. Look at each item and ask yourself if you're avoiding a specific task because you don't know how to do it. If so, you can either delegate it to a co-worker or hire a freelancer to do it for you. However, if you feel like the task is important for your personal development, then you'll need to focus on improving your skills for that task.

Fortunately for you, <u>every</u> task in the world has been successfully completed by someone else. All you have to do is take a proactive approach and educate yourself on how to do it. Here's a six-step process for getting started.

Action I: Identify the specific skill.

First, figure out the exact thing you're trying to learn. For instance, your goal shouldn't be to "become a better public speaker," because that's not an actionable outcome. Instead, it's more effective to have a specific goal in mind that shows you've achieved a certain level of competence.

Using the above example, you could create this goal: "Deliver compelling, step-by-step five-minute YouTube presentations." This is actionable because your success is measurable—either you create the five-minute YouTube videos or you don't.

How you learn something is a lot like developing a project list. Get out a piece of paper and write down every step you'd need to take. Start with your end goal and work your way backward. If there's an unanswered question, then create a task to research it along the way.

Action II: Focus on one skill.

Even if you have a laundry list of things to learn, it's always better to focus on one at a time. Maybe you have a list of "someday" items like running a marathon, learning to juggle, becoming a great public speaker and being a better guitar player. The trick here is to pick the skills that are *immediately* applicable.

You should also think about the impact learning one new skill will have on your life. Using the above example, you might decide to focus on "public speaking" because it could lead to an improvement in job performance, which means more money and an increased capacity to afford fun activities.

Focusing on a single skill is the quickest path to instant competence. While you won't achieve "mastery" overnight, you can learn a lot by concentrating on a single outcome for a few weeks or months.

Action III: Get an education.

I'm sorry to say this, but the traditional model of education is slowly dying away. We currently live in a world that's filled with an abundance of information. All you need is Internet access and a desire to learn. Think of it this way—right now, somebody, somewhere has mastered the skill you're trying to learn. Simply find a person who is kind enough to share their experiences and you'll get a world-class education that can't be found in a traditional classroom setting.

Where can you locate expert advice?

You can get started by checking out the following websites:

- Amazon (http://www.amazon.com) (read books on the subject).
- Google (http://www.google.com)(find information and blogs related to that skill).
- Google Helpouts (https://helpouts.google.com/home)(hire a coach to get instant feedback).
- Udemy (http://www.udemy.com)and Skillfeed (http://www.skillfeed.com)(take an online class on the subject).

- YouTube (http://www.youtube.com)(watch videos that demonstrate a specific concept).
- Facebook (http://www.facebook.com)(connect with authorities who are good at this skill).
- Meetup (http://www.meetup.com)(join local groups interested in this subject).

Information gathering is the most important part of the process. Your goal here is to get good information and listen to the *right* people. Often, it's better to invest a little money with someone who has a proven track record than to follow a "free" tutorial made by a person who has a limited understanding of the topic.

Cast a wide net and get a variety of information on the subject. Don't just listen to one person's opinion. Instead, do a thorough job with your research. Read a few books/magazines on this topic. Talk to people with a variety of expertise. Do everything you can to fully immerse yourself in this skill.

Action IV: Create a step-by-step plan.

This step is also similar to the step-by-step project lists we've already talked about. Whenever you learn something, immediately apply it. You can do this by taking regular "pauses" in your education and implementing what you've learned. In other words, don't get caught in the trap where you procrastinate on something because you feel like you need more information.

Keep adding items to your skill-based project list and then take action. You'll find that the process of applying information is the fastest way to learn a new skill.

Action V: Synthesize your notes.

At a certain point, you'll have learned and applied a wealth of information. The trick is to turn all of this into a simple-to-follow process. At the point where you feel like you've learned the basics, put everything into a single document. This will help you eliminate redundancy and avoid doing tasks that aren't important.

It's not hard to create an actionable collection of notes. Simply get out your trusty three-ring binder and add a section for the skill you're trying to develop. Be sure to include the following:

- **Reference points**: Annotate book page numbers, website links, time markings on important audio/video courses and potential tools to use.

- **Step-by-step blueprints**: Same thing—write down a step-by-step process that's recommended by an expert in that skill. Map out any diagrams or flowcharts.

- **Sticking points**: Write down any questions you have about that skill. If possible, ask someone who has proven expert knowledge.

- **Action items**: Figure out a strategy for what you'll do moving forward. Specifically, create a list of habits you can follow on a daily basis that will bring you one step closer to mastery.

Synthesizing information might seem like busywork, but I feel like it's an important part of the process because it helps you *internalize* what you've learned. You'll find that the process of summarizing and eliminating information helps you develop a deeper understanding of the skill.

Action VI: Take daily action.

Finally, develop the habit of taking action on a daily basis. You could use Lift.do (http://lift.do) to track this new routine. Simply find/create a habit that's related to the skill and then track your daily progress.

It's possible to learn almost anything in the world. The challenge is to find the right information sources and then develop the habit of taking daily action. For more on how to learn skills in a rapid-fire manner, check out *The First 20 Hours* (http://www.developgoodhabits.com/20hours-kindle) by Josh Kaufman.

Once you've applied all of the strategies in the last few chapters, you'll have a list of tasks and habits for each goal. At this point, you'll be ready to take action. So let's talk about how to do that.

Step 6a: Do the Work (or "How Habits Help You Achieve Goals")

By now you've probably noticed something—it's easy to spend a lot of time in the planning phase of setting goals. Unfortunately, some focus way too much time on writing lists and not enough time on *doing the work.*

One of the best lessons I've ever learned about getting things done was from Steven Pressfield's book, *The War of Art* (http://www.developgoodhabits.com/warofartbook). The one truth he emphasized was that successful people in the world don't wait for "events" to achieve a result. Instead, they take consistent action and put in hours of daily effort.

While project lists and mind maps clarify what needs to be accomplished, it's your daily actions that will determine your level of success at achieving a goal. What I recommend is simple. Structure every day so you "do the work" required to achieve each goal. Or to put it differently, you need to turn the day-to-day actions necessary to complete a goal into habits. Here's a six-step plan for doing this:

I. Review your goals: Review your goals on a regular basis. The bare minimum should be once per week, but I actually recommend looking at them first thing in the morning and a couple more times throughout the day. Consistently reading your goals acts as a reminder for why you need to complete certain tasks and how they're tied into your long-term plans.

II. Plan your days: Because you're pursuing multiple goals simultaneously, it's important to block out time for each one. Allocating enough time slots saves you from being overwhelmed by stress.

My advice is to plan your day according to the "Most Important Tasks (MITs)" strategy that I cover in my book *23 Anti-Procrastination Habits* (http://www.developgoodhabits.com/23anti). The idea here is to identify the few actions that will bring you biggest results for the day and then focus on completing them as your first set of tasks.

III. Eliminate time wasters. Getting rid of distractions is just as important as creating an action plan. Some common time wasters include never-ending phone conversations, unannounced visitors, prolonged meetings and new projects that fall into your lap.

The best way to eliminate these distractions is to learn how to say "no" when something doesn't align with your goals (obviously this doesn't include projects that your boss feels are important). When you can quickly identify and avoid the timewasters, you'll free up a lot of time that can be dedicated to achieving a goal.

IV. Use project lists. Develop the habit of creating project lists for every goal. List each action in the correct order and be sure to include any daily habits that are required. Set aside time in the first part of the day for the habit and then schedule other blocks of time to work on specific one-time tasks.

As you work through a project list, ask yourself, "What's the next step?" Say this over and over while working your way through a goal.

V. Get feedback from others. Other people can help during the times when you're not feeling motivated. Find others who share a similar interest and meet up on a regular basis. Talk about the challenges you face and ask for their advice.

If you *can't* find someone like this, talk with your friends, family, spouse or colleagues. This strategy goes back to one of the key components of achieving a goal—the more encouragement you get from others, the more success you'll have with a goal. We'll talk more about this topic in a later section.

VI. Expect setbacks along the way. Achieving goals isn't always easy. Often unexpected events will pop up that derail your efforts. Don't panic when this happens. Simply learn the lesson from the experience and move on.

For instance, you could ask the following when you encounter an obstacle: *How did this happen? Could I prevent it from happening again? Does it open the door for a different opportunity? Does it make me want to stick with my goal? Or does it create a lack of motivation?*

We all experience setbacks. The difference between successful people and the not-so-successful is how they handle them. If you can gain a little bit of knowledge from each "negative" experience, you can use this information to set better goals during the next quarterly review.

Each of these six mini-steps provides the mental framework needed to approach goals on a day-to-day basis. But they don't force you to take action. The real secret to getting things done on a consistent basis is to plan out your weeks and schedule goal-specific activities. In the next section, we'll talk about how to do that.

Step 6b: Use a Weekly Review to Create a Schedule

It's no secret that the best way to achieve a goal is to take daily action. Unfortunately, it's not always easy to consistently work on something—especially when we have a dozen other obligations. The solution is to create a seven-day schedule during a weekly review session.

The weekly review is a concept I originally learned from David Allen's *Getting Things Done* (http://www.developgoodhabits.com/gtd-kindle). It's a simple process. Once a week (I prefer Sundays), look at the next seven days and schedule the activities/projects you'd like to accomplish. In addition, process all the notes from your idea capture mechanism and process any new paperwork.

You can accomplish all of this with three simple steps:

Step #1: Ask Three Questions

When starting a weekly review, ask three questions that will shape the focus of what you'll do over the next seven days:

Q1: What are my personal obligations?

Do I have a planned family activity? Am I going on a vacation? Do I have any personal appointments, meetings or phone calls? Is there something fun I'd like to do?

I've found that it's hard to work on goals when I have a lot of personal obligations. So it's better to *plan* for these potential interruptions rather than have them suddenly pop up and derail the next seven days. Honestly, you'd be better off reducing your output instead of trying to be a superhero by filling each day with 16 hours of activities.

Q2: What are my priority projects?

Sometimes a certain project takes precedence over everything else. This is the time when it's okay to *purposefully* procrastinate on other things. I'm a firm believer in focusing on one thing at a time. You can use the weekly review to focus your efforts on completing a single project that will have the biggest impact on your professional or personal life.

Q3: How much time do I have?

This question is extremely important. If you know your time is limited (like having an upcoming deadline for a specific project), then you should give yourself permission to not begin anything new.

Step #2: Schedule Project Tasks

After answering these three questions, map out the next seven days. The simplest way to do this is to look at the list for each goal and schedule time to follow-up on the most important activities.

Step #3: Process Captured Ideas

If you're like me, you probably write down dozens of great ideas every week. The question is: how do you follow up on them? My advice is to process these notes, making one of two choices: 1) Take action on it immediately or 2) Schedule a time when you'll follow up on it. Here's how that would work:

*I. The idea is actionable.

I'm a big fan of David Allen's "two-minute rule." The idea here is if an idea takes two minutes to complete, then you should do it immediately. No putting it off and no scheduling time for follow-up. *Just do it.*

Now, if an idea is something you'd like to immediately implement, then write out a step-by-step plan for how you'll do it. Simply write down a series of actions you'll take on this idea and then schedule these ideas into your week.

*II. The idea is not actionable.

Sometimes it's not the right time for an idea, but you don't want to forget it. That's when you put the idea into an archive folder that's reviewed every month. If you do this for every idea you have, you won't forget to follow up at the right time.

The weekly review is an important part of achieving your goals. When you plan out each week, you create a sense of urgency, making it more likely you will follow up on each goal. Your weekly review will also help you create a schedule you can turn into a list of daily activities. Let's talk about how to do that in the next section.

Step 6c: Track the Completion of Your Goals

We've already talked about how project plans provide a framework for your long-term goals. The trick here is turning these plans into daily activities. In other words, you need to develop daily habits that can be measured and tracked.

Tracking can be done in a variety of ways. You can do the pen-and-paper approach by recording the successful completion of a habit. Another option is to use software and mobile apps to track your daily activities.

Here are a few popular programs:

1. Lift.do (http://lift.do) is a great program for tracking habits because it's free and available on a variety of platforms including iPhone, Android and desktop computers.

If you can break down a goal into a specific daily habit (like writing, running, not eating carbs, etc.), you can use Lift to measure how often you're following this routine. Simply pick a habit from the thousands included with this tool. Sign up for the app and "check in" whenever you complete a routine. Do this on a daily basis to get encouragement from other members as you successfully work on your goals.

2. GoalSync (http://goalsync.software.informer.com/) is an innovative method of setting daily goals that utilizes subliminal messaging and goal-to-speech technology. What I like best is it emphasizes the use of S.M.A.R.T. goals, so you can rest assured the program is helping you create goals that intelligently fit your lifestyle.

3. AchieveIt (http://www.achieveit.com/) is an excellent software solution for business professionals. If your goals are project-based, this program can help you track and manage them efficiently.

4. ToodleDo (http://www.toodledo.com/info/iphone.php)is an app for iPhone and iPad that focuses on completing specific tasks. It allows you to set multiple goals and associate relevant tasks with each goal. You can create separate action plans for each goal. If you don't have an iPhone/iPad, there is also a Web version (http://www.toodledo.com/).

5. LifeTick (http://lifetick.com/) is another useful application that follows the S.M.A.R.T. goal-setting practice. It is accessible from the Web as well as mobile phones. You can do a lot of things with this program: create daily tasks, set reminders, record

actions in a journal, program personalized tracking and even generate reports to see how many goals you've achieved within a time limit.

6. Goals on Track (http://www.goalsontrack.com/) is a Web-based goal management system. It provides you a detailed form for setting S.M.A.R.T. goals. You can successfully set daily goals, track them and cross them off once they're completed. It offers some fabulous features to prioritize and focus, track time, build goal-enabling habits and keep a daily journal. Mobile apps for iPhone, BlackBerry, Windows Phone 7 and Android-based devices are also available.

7. 42 Goals (http://42goals.com/) is an online resource for tracking your daily goals. It's easy to use and offers two membership levels: free and premium. This tool has customizable templates, icons and some techniques to visually analyze your progress. You can set your daily goals, record your progress and share goals with your friends.

You shouldn't get carried away with using tools to track your goals. My suggestion is to pick one of these seven programs and spend only five minutes each day using your chosen tool. At the end of each day, do the following:
Update your progress by recording the habits you've successfully completed.

- Record the progress you've made on individual goals.

- Write down the actions you'd like to complete for the next day.

Taking action on your goals isn't hard when you chunk everything down into a daily routine. Simply identify the tasks you need to complete, schedule time to complete each task and track your progress. Consistently using this simple process is the best way to take massive action on all of your goals.

We've already talked about *three types* of obstacles that often pop up during a mind-mapping session. Some of these obstacles are really caused by internal fears and beliefs, but there are times you'll encounter legitimate problems that could prevent you from achieving a goal. That means you'll need to create a plan for how you'll deal with them. We'll cover that in the next section.

Step 7: Overcome Five Obstacles to S.M.A.R.T. Goal Setting

Achieving goals might seem like a simplistic process: you write down a desired outcome, work hard for a few months and then achieve the goal. Seems simple, right? Unfortunately, many people fail because they don't account for those random challenges that often come out of left field.

Specifically there are five primary obstacles. Here they are—each with a possible solution:

Obstacle #1: Life Gets in the Way

There's an old military adage that says, *"The best battle plan is good until the first bullet is fired."*

The point here is simple—you can map out the perfect plan for achieving a goal, but it won't last that long once you get real-world feedback.

Let's face it…we all get sidetracked when random events fall into our laps. Whether it's an emergency, an exciting project, a change of plans or even a new goal, we all have those moments when our goals get derailed due to an unexpected change in our lives.

The solution?

There is one thing that successful goal achievers do that others do not. They understand that random events often occur, so they plan for them and create a strategy for how they'll respond.

One possible strategy is to create an "If-Then Plan." (http://www.developgoodhabits.com/if-then-plan/) The idea here is to understand the situations that make you deviate from your original plan and then create a plan for how you'll handle them.

An if-then plan sounds like this: *"If X happens, then I'll do Y."*

Take a look at each of the goals on your list. Ask yourself what causes you to slip or not follow through with your commitments. Then create a series of "if-then statements" for how you'll handle these random events. Rinse and repeat until you've established an action plan to handle the obstacles for each goal.

Obstacle #2: You Don't Have Motivation

Why am I a fan of the three-month goal strategy? One of my reasons is it's easy to stay motivated for a goal when it's just over the horizon. Sometimes though, immediacy isn't a good enough reason for sticking with a goal. Instead, it's easy for people to give up because they're simply no longer interested in that outcome.

The solution?

Experiencing a lack of motivation is extremely damaging to the long-term success of <u>all</u> your goals. Fortunately, there are two quick fixes for this problem.

First, you can eliminate the goal. You created it, so there's nothing wrong with realizing a goal isn't working and then eliminating it.

The problem with motivation is a single "goal failure" can often cause a negative chain reaction to affect every goal on your list. If you're not inspired by a certain outcome, then it's easy to carry that feeling into everything else you're trying to accomplish.

If you're feeling resistant to working on a goal, then take time to decide if it's really worth the effort. If not, then get rid of it and focus on an alternative goal.

The second solution is to celebrate specific accomplishments and milestones. It's easy to get dragged down by the daily drudgery of going after a long-term goal. Usually this happens when a major accomplishment requires willpower on a daily basis (like writing, exercising and eating healthy). Some people are so focused on the end prize that they don't take time to smell the proverbial roses.

You can overcome this obstacle by creating mini-milestones (like one each week) and celebrating each accomplishment. This celebration doesn't have to be a big event. Simply treat yourself to an extra hour of T.V. or a trip to the spa. The key here is to get into the practice of enjoying those small successes.

Obstacle #3: Too Many Goals, Too Little Time

Another challenge is to avoid bouncing from one goal to another without making genuine progress. This often happens because plans are exciting, but *doing* them requires discipline. The end result is many people become experts at making plans without taking consistent action on them.

The Solution?

First, it's important to pare down your list to a maximum of five goals. This will prevent you from being pulled in a million different directions.

Once you've established this list, focus on your goals using a top-down approach. Make sure to start each day by focusing on the #1 goal and then scheduling time for the other four. *When* you do each depends on your schedule. The important thing is to prioritize what truly matters and spend the majority of your time on these activities.

Finally, it's important to understand where each goal fits in your life. Ask yourself these questions: *Is this project meaningful? How does it fit in with my long-term plans? Am I missing out on other things by focusing on it? Is there a better goal I could pursue?*

Ask these questions on a regular basis (I recommend once a week) to gain clarity on your goals. If you find that a particular goal keeps getting pushed aside, then that's a strong indicator you need to change or eliminate it.

Obstacle #4: Experiencing Consistent Failure

It's easy to give up on a goal when all you're seeing is failure. Either you've made a major mistake or a negative event popped up. The end result is the same: your plan for achieving an outcome has turned into a failure.

Often, this obstacle is the worst of the bunch because while the *desire* is still there, your efforts aren't generating results.

The Solution?

I recommend a two-step process for overcoming those moments of failure.

First you need to re-commit to the goal.

Often a major obstacle means a goal is no longer worth pursuing. Perhaps it will take too much time, money or effort to overcome. Maybe your desire has hit rock bottom. Or perhaps the goal is more grueling than you originally anticipated.

If *any* of these things happen, then you should take time to see if it's worth continuing with the goal (like you would do with obstacle #2). If you've completely lost the drive to continue, then it's okay to change plans and do something different.

Second, if you *do* want to continue with a goal, then focus on learning a lesson from this obstacle. Ask yourself these questions: *What went wrong? Is there something I could have done differently? Does this failure open the door for a new opportunity? What should I do moving forward?*

You can learn a lot by examining a specific obstacle. In fact, an obstacle often provides more long-term value than the successful achievement of a goal. Since I'm a big nerd, I'll end with a line from *Game of Thrones*: *"A bruise is a lesson... and each lesson makes us better."*

Obstacle #5: _____ Says Your Goal Will Fail

We often encounter resistance from other people when they hear about our goals. This resistance usually takes one of two forms. The first is when someone who genuinely cares about you makes a comment that triggers your doubts and makes you question your goals. The other is when someone tells you flat out you will fail. Maybe the person is jealous of you, or maybe he thinks your success will hurt his self-image. No matter the reason, some people will try to derail your progress before you even get started.

The reason "why" someone makes a negative comment is irrelevant. What *does* matter is their words can have a devastating impact on your psyche. Often we sabotage our efforts because it's easy to believe the negative feedback we get from others.

The Solution?

It's important to first understand the underlying reason behind each piece of criticism. That way, you'll know what response is appropriate.

The first type of criticism can be helpful because it identifies potential obstacles. If someone raises a consideration you initially didn't anticipate, then you can use it as an opportunity to create a plan for how you'll handle the potential obstacle. This goes back to obstacle #1. When you have a solid "if-then plan" for each situation, you'll be fully prepared to respond if it ever occurs.

The second type of criticism comes from people who aren't happy with your desire to improve yourself. These are the friends, family members and co-workers who act like they have your best interests at heart, but often say things that are hurtful—even detrimental to your success.

How do you handle this type of person?

If it's someone who is a permanent part of your life (like a family member), then avoid talking about your goals around them. You can still enjoy being around them. The difference is you won't share that side of your personality.

On the other hand, you'll often talk to negative people who aren't really part of your inner circle. My advice? Stop spending time with them. Life is too short to be around people whose biggest export is negativity. Get these people out of your life and find others who share your passion for a specific goal.

Now, we've talked at length about taking action and overcoming obstacles. While these actions are crucial for your success, it's equally important to review goals on a daily basis. This is how you stay motivated and inspired. In the next section, we'll go over a few simple strategies for reviewing goals on a consistent basis.

Step 8: Review Your Goals

It's easy to forget about your goals if you don't review them on a daily basis. Setting aside time for a daily review is one of the most important things you can do to improve the likelihood of reaching a goal. It doesn't matter how busy you are. If you are not reviewing your goals every day, you will be less likely to succeed.

As we've discussed, obstacles often get in the way of our goals. Sometimes you lose the passion and the drive to push forward on your long-term plans. My advice? Review your goals *at least* one to three times per day.

How do you "review" goals?

Here's a simple process that I follow:

1. Take out your list of goals.
2. Read each goal slowly and read it out loud.
3. Pause, close your eyes and visualize the feeling of achieving each goal.
4. Repeat this procedure for each goal.
5. Dedicate five minutes of your day to this habit.

Reviewing a goal isn't a simple matter of looking at a goal and imagining a perfect version of you. What you need to do is turn this activity into a regular routine. Here are three strategies that can help.

Strategy 1: Anchor Goals to an Existing Habit

We all follow certain daily routines like eating a bowl of cereal in the morning, watching the evening news or taking your dog for a walk. You don't have to "force" yourself to do any of these things because they're ingrained habits. The good news here is you can take these routines and anchor them with the review habit.

For instance, let's say you decide to combine "goal review time" with your meals. You'd do this by setting a reminder (with a mobile app like Mind Jogger [http://bit.ly/1hpPl8S]) to do this activity *before* eating. When the alarm goes off, you'd pull out your goals book and spend five minutes reviewing each goal. If you do this for a few weeks, it'll become an ingrained habit to review your goals prior to each meal.

Strategy 2: Carry Goals with You

One of the easiest ways to follow through with the review habit is to carry your goal list wherever you go. Try recording goals in a variety of formats so you have constant, instant access to this list.

For example, your goals should be in the following places:

1. A three-ring binder

2. On a sheet of paper that's kept in your car

3. As a list on your mobile phone

4. Within a folder on apps like <u>Evernote</u> and <u>Dropbox</u>

5. On 3-inch by 5-inch cards that you keep on you

6. On a small sheet of paper that's in your wallet

7. As a note on your desk, refrigerator and bedside table

8. As a note on your most-used desktop applications (iGoogle, Microsoft Outlook, Firefox, etc)

You don't necessarily have to do everything on this list. The important thing is to make sure your goals are always in front of your eyes or at your fingertips.

Strategy 3: Create Goal Reminders

Another thing that helps is to create reminders that help you stick with a goal. These should be strategically placed in prominent locations. Here are a few ways to do this:

I. Visual Reminders: Visual stimulation can be an excellent source of inspiration. One trick is to take old magazines and cut out images/keywords that relate to your goals; pin these images to a board. Keep this board in a frequently used location—like your home office.

There are two ways you can expand on this idea: 1. Make more than one board for each room with different goals. 2. Add goal-related images as a background for your desktop computer or cell phone.

The important point here is to add images in as many places as possible.

II. Pointed Notes: A *pointed note* is a powerful device to nudge you in the direction of working on a goal.

For example, if you're trying to master ten yoga postures as a three-month goal, you can post a pointed note such as, *"What have you done today to master your yoga posture?"*

Another example, if you are trying to follow a diet plan, is to post notes saying, "No Fast Food Today." This is something I did a few months back while trying to kick my fast food habit (http://www.developgoodhabits.com/no-fast-food/).

III. The Progress Bar: A progress bar is great for showing a graphical representation of how far you've come on a specific goal. It's another way to add a visual element to all the hard work you've done.

For example, let's say you have this goal: "By April 1, I want to have a total of $20,000 in my savings account that will be used as a down payment on a house."

You could create a progress bar with $0 as the starting point and $20,000 as the end point. Between these points, draw lines that show increments of $500. For each $500 milestone, you color the bar indicating your progress. Again, you can hang this progress bar in the rooms where you spend most of your time.

It's easy to create a progress bar using a large piece of graph paper. You can also use Excel if you prefer to do things on your computer. Here is a tutorial that shows you how to do this: http://bit.ly/1o0NYiV

IV. Email Reminders: Google Calendar (https://www.google.com/calendar) is a useful tool for setting appointments and creating email reminders. You can also use it to schedule a goal reminder on a daily basis or every few hours.

Another way to use this tool is to set reminders about specific goals. That means every day, you'll get an email that prompts you into taking action. Done correctly, this will act as a positive trigger to keep working on your goals.

V. Accountability Partner(s): It can be really motivating to meet with a friend who shares a desire to achieve a similar goal. You each share your experiences and learn from one another. Specifically you could talk about your successes, breakthroughs, lessons learned and strategies you hope to eliminate.

An additional benefit of an accountability partner is you can perform daily tasks together (like exercising) and encourage one another. Most importantly, your accountability partner is there whenever you feel a slip in motivation or productivity. Sometimes even a simple "nudge" by a trusted friend can be enough to help you stop making excuses and start taking action.

Reviewing goals is one of the secrets to staying motivated. It's easy to get sidetracked when you're being pulled in a million different directions. However, if you dedicate a little bit of time every day to review your goals, your mind will be infused with a constant reminder about what's *really* important in life.

That said, sometimes a daily review session doesn't provide enough motivation to stick with a goal.

Instead, you need to get outside help in maintaining that goal momentum. In the next step, we'll talk about how to do this.

Step 9: Use Accountability to Stay Motivated

There is a strong connection between goals and motivation. Goal setting guides a person in achieving their desired outcomes, while motivation provides the psychological inspiration needed to take action. You are more likely to take consistent action if you have a true sense of purpose while you work to achieve a goal. Your motivation gives you that sense of purpose.

Motivation is essential because it sparks both the physical and mental stimulation necessary to achieve your goals. If your goals are motivating, you feel energized enough to stay committed, work hard and perform tasks in an efficient manner.

Why Do People Feel Unmotivated?

It's surprising how often we feel unmotivated to do a specific activity—even if we know it's directly related to an important goal. There are a few possible reasons why you often get this feeling with a task:

- It doesn't relate to a specific dream or aspiration.
- It's poorly defined and doesn't have a specific outcome.
- It doesn't have an actionable plan for its achievement.
- It's imposed upon you by someone else.
- It's no longer related to an important goal.

You'll find that motivation is at its highest level when you work on goals that are realistic, attainable and in harmony with your core values.

Accountability = Motivation

It's impossible to be consistently motivated if you're doing things in an isolated setting. It doesn't matter if you're a "strong-willed" person; we all have those moments of doubt and hesitation. The solution? Find an accountability partner who can keep you focused on important goals.

When you have an accountability partner, you meet and talk about your goals on a regular basis. You can be 100 percent honest about your failures and successes when you talk to your accountability partner. During each session, you share ideas, talk about your successes and failures, and bounce ideas off one another.

As an example, Tom Ewer (from Leaving Work Behind [http://www.leavingworkbehind.com]) is my accountability partner. Each Wednesday, we talk on Skype for 30 to 60 minutes about our goals and current projects. At the end of each session, we make a commitment to complete specific tasks by the following Wednesday. If one of us doesn't follow through, the other person is there to give a motivational "kick in the butt." For more on this, read his article about mastermind groups (http://www.leavingworkbehind.com/mastermind-group).

How to Find an Accountability Partner

Finding an accountability partner doesn't have to be a difficult process. My suggestion is to look for a person who has all (or at least most) of these qualities:

1. Similar goals or interests
2. Familiar with the focus of your goals
3. Positive, driven and persistent
4. Reliable enough to meet on a weekly or bi-weekly basis
5. Strong-willed enough to (nicely) kick you in the butt if you're slacking

Who this person is depends on the nature of your goals. It can be a friend, family member, colleague or even someone you've met on the Internet. For instance, Tom and I connected through our blogs. While I've never met him in person, I completely trust his advice because we share a mutual desire to build a successful, content-based Internet business.

There are a lot of places to find a great accountability partner: local clubs, business groups, Meetup.com, activity centers (gyms, libraries, etc.), paid weekend events (like an investing seminar) and interest-specific Web forums.

How to Run an Accountability Session

Don't let the word "accountability" make you nervous. Usually these meetings are pretty informal; you each share your experiences and talk about what you'd like to accomplish. That said, here are a few ground rules to make sure both people get the most out of each session:

I. Understand your communication preference: Both people should be clear about what they like and don't like when receiving feedback. Specifically, when it comes to not completing a specific task, how will you support one another? Do you prefer bluntness where the other person calls you out? Or do you like a gentler, kinder approach?

Typically, it's best to match yourself with someone who shares a similar style of communication. This will reduce the risk of getting your feelings hurt or mistakenly saying the wrong thing.

II. Create an accountability appointment: Decide how you'll regularly communicate. If you meet in person, pick a location. If you're talking online, decide on your preferred Web tool (Skype [http://www.skype.com]vs. Google Hangouts [http://www.google.com/+/learnmore/hangouts/]).

Equally important: pick *when* you'll meet. Is it once a week or once a month? What time works for both of you? Is this a time/date that works for both of you on a permanent basis? At first, you'll probably test different days and times, but eventually you'll find the time that works for both of you.

III. Pick people based on shared interests: An accountability partner should share an interest in a specific goal. You want someone who understands your unique challenges and can share their experiences. This means if you have multiple goals that are equally important, then you'll want to meet with multiple accountability partners.

EXAMPLE:

I've already talked about my accountability sessions with Tom. Besides our meetings, I also occasionally show up at a regular run with marathoners who live in my area. While we don't talk about goals per se, we all share similar experiences of having to train for a challenging race. This group run is an excellent motivator for those times when I'm not in the mood to exercise.

When to Join a Mastermind Group

An alternative to working with an accountability partner is to find a mastermind group. The advantage here is you get multiple perspectives on your problem. The disadvantage is you won't get a lot of time to go over your problems and obstacles.

What is a mastermind group?

Basically it's a group of people who:

1. Pursue the same goals or interests.
2. Brainstorm ideas, share important lessons and provide feedback on how to move forward when feeling stuck.

3. Are self-motivated, passionate and proactive about their goals.

4. Help each other reach their goals by sharing their wisdom and expertise.

5. Provide honest feedback on your progress.

6. Have knowledge, skills, ability and proven results in the field of your interest.

7. Share resources, tools and referrals.

8. Offer a different perspective that you might not get from others.

9. Hold you accountable for following through with a goal.

Mastermind groups require more commitment than an accountability partner, but they can offer exponential results because you can "crowdsource" ideas for any problem you're experiencing. If you find that you work better in a group setting, then you might find it's better to find (or form) a group of people who share your interests.

When to Hire a Coach

A professional coach can also help with the achievement of S.M.A.R.T. goals. In a way, a coach is like a good psychologist. He or she acts as a sounding board and gives you feedback about what to do next. The best coaches will help you identify crucial mistakes *before* they spiral out of control. They give advice about how to overcome problems and usually provide a kick in the butt if you're slacking off.

There are two types of coaches:

The first focuses on a specific area of your life (running, public speaking, financial, etc.). Not only will this person act as a mentor, they also provide quality information because they've already accomplished many of the goals you're trying to achieve.

The second is the life coach who can motivate you in multiple areas of your life. Not only does this person act as a mentor, they will help you find that balance that many people miss when they're trying to do too much.

While both options are good, I recommend picking a coach based on a specific goal. My reason? By hiring a skill-based coach, you not only get good feedback for certain problems, you also get to tap into their deep knowledge about a particular topic.

How Do You Find a Coach?

You can find a qualified coach in a variety of places:

- Knowledge-for-hire services like Google Helpouts (https://helpouts.google.com/)
- Local organizations and groups
- Niche-specific blogs (look at their "About" sections to see if the bloggers offer coaching services)
- Referrals from people in your accountability/mastermind groups
- Social media: Connect with authorities on the subject and see if they offer coaching

As you can see, there are a number of ways other people can help you stay motivated. You could get feedback from a regular one-on-one meeting or you could join an organized group. You could even hire a professional to coach you through specific problems.

The choice is up to you. You'll find that as you work through your goals, you'll start to notice where you're lacking. If you don't know how to do something, then a coach is the best option. If you find that you need consistent feedback from a like-minded person, then you should find an accountability partner. And if you need a fun, motivational environment, then it's best to join a mastermind group.

Up to this point, we've covered a wealth of information about creating and achieving goals. Eventually you'll reach the three-month mark when it's time to evaluate your progress. Did you succeed or fail? What lessons did you learn? Are there new goals you'd like to add? All of these questions will be answered in the next chapter.

Step 10: Do a Goal Evaluation Every Three Months

You work hard on your goals every day. You even review them on a weekly and daily basis. The problem? Some people never take a step back and understand the "why" behind each goal. In other words, people don't review their goals to see if they're *actually* worth pursuing. That's why it's important to have a goal evaluation every three months.

What's the point of a three-month evaluation? It acts like a quarterly report of your long-term S.M.A.R.T. goals. First, you'll measure the progression of your long-term outcomes. Then you'll take a look at how your daily actions match your expectations. And finally you end with an action plan for the next three months.

You can complete a three-month evaluation by asking a few simple questions:

- Have I attained the desired outcome?
- What were the successful *and* unsuccessful strategies?

- Did I put 100 percent of my effort toward completing these goals? If not, why?
- Have I achieved results consistent with my efforts?
- Why should I continue to focus on this goal for the next three-months?
- What goals should I eliminate or alter?
- What goals should I add?
- Is there anything new I'd like to try?

Even though it takes a few hours to complete this evaluation, you should always take time do it every quarter. It will be your ultimate safeguard against wasting time on a goal that *doesn't* align with your long-term plans.

How to Do a Three-Month Evaluation

It's not hard to perform an evaluation. Here's a simple action plan that I recommend:

1. Dedicate a few hours on a day when you can work in isolation.
2. Go through each goal. Look at the metrics to see if it was successfully completed.
3. Examine the strategies that helped you succeed. Is there any way you can do more of these activities?
4. Figure out why you failed with certain goals. Was it due to a lack of motivation or a specific obstacle? What do you know now that you would have done differently?
5. Identify the primary obstacles. What will you do in the future to overcome them?

6.   Generate ideas for improvement. Think of different ways you could have improved the process.

7.   Repeat this process for each goal.

8.   Identify the goals that are no longer relevant. Can you change the wording and focus on a similar goal? If it's no longer important, then get rid of it.

9.   Pull out your life list. Does any idea spark your interest? If so, turn it into a S.M.A.R.T. goal and add it to the list.

10. Create a new set of goals for the next quarter. Use everything you've learned during this evaluation to create outcomes that are both motivational and inspiring.

The three-month evaluation is about learning from past experiences. It's not the time to be cocky because of a few successes or beat yourself up if you've failed. Instead, it should provide a learning experience for you to take everything that happened in the last quarter and apply it to the milestones you'd like to achieve in the future.

Conclusion

Our time together is at an end. You now possess a blueprint for setting dynamic S.M.A.R.T. goals and achieving them on a consistent basis. If you can clearly define what you want with a series of actionable steps, then it's possible to reach any challenging milestone.

Like I do with every book, I urge you to take action. The reason I've included phrases like "steps," "strategies" and "action plans" is because I want you to immediately implement this information. In other words, you won't achieve *any* goal by simply reading a book. Real results come from the real-world application of knowledge.

You've learned a ten-step process for achieving S.M.A.R.T. goals. To help you put this information into action, let me recap with a simple step-by-step process:

- Step 1: Buy a goal book.
- Step 2: Create a life list for the seven areas of your life.

- Step 3: Write down goals you want to achieve between now and the end of the year.
- Step 4a: Focus on the next three months and pick challenging goals.
- Step 4b: Write down five (or fewer) quarterly goals in the S.M.A.R.T. format.
- Step 5a: Turn each quarterly goal into an action plan.
- Step 5b: Brainstorm additional tasks using mind mapping.
- Step 5c: Learn the required skills for each goal.
- Step 6a: Commit to working on your goal every single day.
- Step 6b: Create a schedule with a weekly review.
- Step 6c: Track the completion of your goals with apps and software.
- Step 7: Learn to overcome the five major goal-setting obstacles.
- Step 8: Review your goals on a daily basis.
- Step 9: Find an accountability partner or group to stay motivated.
- Step 10: Evaluate your goal progression every three months.

S.M.A.R.T. goals can have an amazing impact on your life. They provide motivation throughout the day and a sense of direction if you're struggling with a particular habit. When you have a clear idea of what's important, you can make smart decisions (pun intended) about what to do on a daily basis.

It's okay if you fail with a particular goal. Just treat each failure as an opportunity to learn something new. The important thing is to redefine the internal boundaries of what you think is possible and can be accomplished in your life.

If you consistently apply the principles of S.M.A.R.T. goal setting to your life, you will have the opportunity to achieve any goal you desire. Whether you want to earn a six-figure income, run your first marathon or simply lose a few pounds, S.M.A.R.T. goals can help you get there.

Steve Scott
http://www.DevelopGoodHabits.com

Would You Like to Know More?

Often it's easy to procrastinate on going after your goals. You ignore them because you're paralyzed by uncertainty and what's required to make things happen in your life.

One way to fix this problem is to adopt an "anti-procrastination" mindset. When you know *how* to take action on a consistent basis, you can systematically accomplish any goal. In my book, *23 Anti-Procrastination Habits*, you'll get a series of simple-to-follow routines that can help not only achieve your goals, but can increase your productivity in many different areas.

You can learn more here
http://www.developgoodhabits.com/book-23aph

Thank You

Before you go, I'd like to say "thank you" for purchasing my guide.

I know you could have picked from dozens of books on habit development, but you took a chance with my system.

So a big thanks for ordering this book and reading all the way to the end.

Now I'd like ask for a *small* favor. Could you please take a minute or two and leave a review for this book on Amazon? http://amzn.to/1hGrao0

This feedback will help me continue to write the kind of books that help you get results. And if you loved it, then please let me know :-)

More Books by S.J. Scott

- *23 Anti-Procrastination Habits: How to Stop Being Lazy and Get Results In Your Life*

- *Writing Habit Mastery: How to Write 2,000 Words a Day and Forever Cure Writer's Block*

- *Declutter Your Inbox: 9 Provem Steps to Eliminate Email Overload*

- *Wake Up Successful: How to Increase Your Energy and Achieve Any Goal with a Morning Routine*

- *10,000 Steps Blueprint: The Daily Walking Habit for Healthy Weight Loss and Lifelong Fitness*

- *70 Healthy Habits: How to Eat Better, Feel Great, Get More Energy and Live a Healthy Lifestyle*

- *Resolutions That Stick! How 12 Habits Can Transform Your New Year*

About the Author

"Build a Better Life - One Habit at a Time"

Getting more from life doesn't mean following the latest diet craze or motivation program. True success happens when you take action on a daily basis. In other words, it's your habits that help you achieve goals and live the life you've always wanted.

In his books, S.J. provides daily action plans for every area of your life: health, fitness, work and personal relationships. Unlike other personal development guides, his content focuses on taking action. So instead of reading over-hyped strategies that rarely work in the real-world, you'll get information that can be immediately implemented

When not writing, S.J. likes to read, exercise and explore the different parts of the world.